Charles Darwin

by Anna Sproule

Published in Great Britain in 1990
by Exley Publications Ltd,
16 Chalk Hill, Watford,
Herts WD1 4BN, United Kingdom.

Copyright © Exley Publications, 1990
Reprinted 1993.

British Library Cataloguing in Publication Data
Sproule, Anna.
    Charles Darwin – (Scientists
    who have changed the world).
    1.   Organisms. Evolution.
        Darwin, Charles *1809-82*.
    I.   Title.
    II.   Series.
    575.0092'4

ISBN 1-85015-213-6

Series editor: Helen Exley.
Picture research: Veneta Bullen and Kate Duffy.
Editing: Margaret Montgomery.
Typeset by Brush Off Studios,
St Albans, Herts AL3 4PH.
Printed and bound in Hungary.

Charles Darwin

*The story of how the Theory of Evolution
completely changed our view of natural history*

Anna Sproule

 EXLEY

Too late

He was too late. His life's work had gone for nothing. The black land and its mysteries, the years of research, the endless sifting of fact after fact: what did it all count for now?

It was twenty-three years since Charles Darwin, naturalist and future country gentleman, had started his great hunt for the truth. And he'd found it. He knew that, as well as he knew his own name. If only he'd managed to finish the book he was writing! If only he'd been less painstaking, less anxious to cover every possible quibble or objection. But it was all over now.

A rival had arrived at the truth as well: a rival who would soon tell the world what he'd discovered. A rival who – Heaven help them both – had come to him for friendship and help.

As, stooped and grim-faced, Darwin plodded on his midday walk, he knew he was facing the greatest crisis of his life.

The black land

Sweet and heady, the scents of early summer drifted past his nostrils. But he paid them no attention. In his mind, he was far from the English countryside, and years away from 1858.

He was in a place where the Pacific Ocean's waves broke endlessly on a scorching black beach. On black rocks too hot for a man to touch, big dark lizards sprawled in luxury. Monstrous tortoises ambled by, munching cactus. Above them, perched on the cactus spines, small birds twittered. Over everything hung a harsh, heavy smell, as if the dry scrub were on fire.

Lords of the black land: in the Galapagos Islands, a marine iguana (opposite) surveys its rock-lined habitat, while a giant tortoise (below) paces through the island scrub. Their ancestors, 150 years ago, set Charles Darwin on the path to a discovery that would completely change the way the world thought.

5

He was back where, in 1835, it had all begun: in the Galapagos Islands. In Spanish, he remembered, they were also called the Enchanted Isles. Enchanted? While he was there, someone had said they looked like hell itself.

So, hell was where it had all started. And hell was where he was now.

The making of new species

The Enchanted Isles and their black rocks faded from Darwin's tormented mind. In their place came other, newer memories: the drawing room a few hours ago, and the little heap of letters waiting for him. Among them was one from the East Indies. It had been sent by fellow-naturalist Alfred Russel Wallace.

Wallace's letter felt heavy. Cheerfully, Darwin had ripped it open, pulled out the thick wad of pages it contained, and sat down to read them. As he read, his contentment fell around him in ruins.

But, far away in the Moluccas, Wallace sounded cheerful enough for two. He had been ill with malaria. That was over, however. And, while he was sweating and shivering in its grip, he had had the most amazing idea: a flash of inspiration. He had worked out how different kinds of living things, or species, were created.

Struggling to survive

All living things, Wallace had realized, faced a life-or-death struggle for survival. They were hunted; they fell ill; they starved. Dangers like these threatened all species and, within a single species, threatened all its members. So why did some die, and others live?

The answer lay in the small differences that occurred between organisms that were otherwise similar. For instance, the fastest animals in a group could outrun their enemies. The most intelligent could outwit them. And the healthiest – the strongest and best fed – could shake off diseases that killed weaker group members. Only the best-equipped for survival stood much chance of living.

"Let us take the case of a wolf, which preys on various animals, securing some by craft, some by strength, and some by fleetness; and let us suppose that the fleetest prey, a deer for instance, had from any change in the country increased in numbers, or that other prey had decreased in numbers, during that season of the year when the wolf was hardest pressed for food. Under such circumstances the swiftest and slimmest wolves would have the best chance of surviving and so be preserved or selected...."

Charles Darwin, from "The Origin of Species".

Their young had a better chance of survival too. They might well inherit their parents' unusual speed, cunning or strength. And so might their children, and their children's children.... Very slowly, new varieties of animals emerged: new types, in which all the animals shared some special, extra quality that aided survival.

So there it was: four thousand words of explanation and argument, written in a feverish frenzy of inspiration. The cat's claws, the falcon's great talons, the long neck with which the giraffe reached high into trees for its food: Wallace's theory covered them all. Although written so fast, his paper was quite ready for other scientists to read and assess; in fact, it was ready for publication.

Did Darwin think it was any good?

The old friends

Under the cool trees, Darwin realized he was sweating. Of course he thought Wallace's work was good. It was admirable. He understood it as well as if he'd written it himself. Every idea, every link in the argument: he knew them all like old friends.

"Those that prolong their existence can only be the most perfect in health and vigour; ... the weakest and least perfectly organized must always succumb."
Alfred Russel Wallace, from the paper read to the Linnean Society in 1858.

Darwin's country home and the scene of the greatest crisis of his life: Down House, Downe, now on the borders of London. He moved there in 1842, six years after his return from the Galapagos, to get away from the bustle and social distractions of the capital. Completely immersed in his work and his family, he lived there until his death in 1882.

And why not? He'd been living with them for years. In their haziest form, he'd been living with them ever since he had seen the Enchanted Isles and their strange inhabitants.

Wallace had had his great idea about the struggle for survival just a short while ago, in 1858. He, Darwin, had reached the same basic conclusions in the late 1830s – but only a few people knew.

He'd first roughed out his own "species theory" in 1842, and he'd been working on it ever since: expanding, confirming, polishing. His friends kept urging him to make his ideas public, to write a book, and, two years ago, he'd even started. It was going to be a big book. It had to be, to get in all the facts he'd collected to support his hypothesis of "natural selection": the way in which nature itself

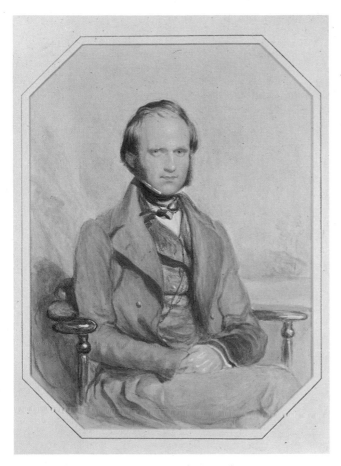

Charles Darwin in 1840, when he was thirty-one. Outwardly, he still looked much like the fit, energetic young man who had voyaged to the other side of the world. But he was already beginning to suffer from the ill health that would dog him for the rest of his life. He had also reached the basic conclusions of his "species theory". People have wondered ever since whether his revolutionary ideas and his illness were in some way linked.

works to bring new species into existence.

It was his life's work; his child. He wanted it to be perfect. And now.... The scientific world worked just like the natural one. Success went to the quickest off the mark, the first to publish.

Wallace, not Darwin.

How could he bear it?

What made it worse was that Wallace had come to Darwin for assistance. Wallace trusted him to send the paper on to another scientist, the influential geologist Sir Charles Lyell. How could he let his fellow-naturalist down? If he did, he would be guilty of the worst form of double-dealing; he would be

"I happened to read for amusement Malthus on 'Population', and being well prepared to appreciate the struggle for existence which everywhere goes on from long-continued observation of the habits of animals and plants, it at once struck me that under these circumstances favourable variations would tend to be preserved, and unfavourable ones to be destroyed. The result of this would be the formation of new species."

Charles Darwin.

betraying a trust to further his own ends.

He couldn't bear it. The manuscript must go off to Sir Charles at once, today. It was the right thing to do – the only thing. And, after that, he would not be able to publish his own views. His life's work would soon become a footnote to someone else's published ideas. He was not sure he could bear that either.

Suddenly, under his feet, Darwin realized he could feel pebbles rather than grass. He'd come back to the house. Wearily, he pushed open the tall glass door, and made his way inside.

The book that changed the world

Darwin never finished his "big book". But neither did he have to give up his life's work, and the reputation that deserved to go with it. In agonies of conscience, he was quite ready to let Wallace take all the credit for the species theory. But Lyell and Darwin's other friends managed to stop him just in time. Then they arranged for his own early sketch to be presented, together with Wallace's paper, at a meeting of top-level British scientists.

They all realized that there was now no time to lose. Wallace, they knew, might soon produce a book himself. Darwin *had* to come up with his own worked-out findings on natural selection as quickly as possible. If he didn't hurry, his chances would be finished for good.

Darwin did hurry. Before the summer was out, he had started writing a much shorter, simpler version of the longer work. It still took him nearly a year but this, for Darwin, was lightning-fast. And, on November 24, 1859, the "book of the book" was published. Called *The Origin of Species,* it changed the world.

Pigeons, fossils and cows

At first glance, a modern reader might find it hard to see why. The book ranges far and wide over many aspects of biology, the science of living things. The first chapter, for instance, looks at the breeding of domestic plants and animals: roses, strawberries, cows, pigeons. The third and fourth introduce the

The four types of beak shown here all belong to different species of Galapagos Island finch. Differences like these helped Darwin work out his theory of evolution.

10

ideas at the heart of Darwin's thinking; the struggle for existence in the wild, the survival of the best-equipped, and the whole process of natural selection that leads to the evolution of new species. But other chapters look at animal instincts and at geology and fossils.

Shaped by a great designer?

Today, the idea of evolution seems ordinary, almost self-evident. Most of us take it for granted. In the world of science, obviously, the person who first worked the idea out must have caused a stir – but in the world of science only. So why should a book on the way living things evolve be so important?

The answer lies in the way people in Europe then thought of living things, themselves included. In the nineteenth century, the world was dominated by the Christian nations of the West. So was the world's thinking. And most Christians believed that the world's creatures and plants were, quite literally, the work of God. They had been shaped once and for all by a divine designer, during the six days after

Many religions are founded on the idea of a divine designer. Above, a "designer" of the Ancient Greeks, the harvest goddess Demeter, sends a charioteer to earth with instructions on how to plant her great gift of corn. In Babylonian mythology, the world was created out of Chaos, or nothingness, by the god Marduk. The Babylonian story was already old when the Bible's account of the world's creation was written.

he first created the world itself.

Many Christians, in fact, were also quite sure about the date of the world's creation. God had brought it into being on October 23, 4004 BC – or so two clergymen had calculated. And all believers knew that, in God's scheme of things, human beings like themselves played a special role.

Like other creatures, they, too, were the work of God. But, as the Bible taught, they had been shaped by God "in his own image". Unlike any other living thing, they shared something of God's own power and glory.

A formula for revolution

Darwin's book, however, demolished these ideas. It removed God – a benevolent, caring God – from the picture. It also removed all idea of purposeful, once-and-for-all design. Instead, it said that living things were constantly changing, evolving, being re-shaped: re-shaped in blood and misery, by the heedless forces of nature. "Survival of the fittest", Darwin's other name for his natural selection theory, was a much harsher creed than the one with which most Christians comforted themselves: "Father-like, He tends and spares us".

And, at the very end of his book, Darwin had even included a hint that humans – far from being special – were as subject to the laws of natural selection as anything else.

To believing Christians everywhere, the implications of Darwin's great theory were world-shattering. If he was right, all their views on the universe and their own place in it simply fell apart. When *The Origin* was published, it naturally caused a hurricane of furious – and terrified – protest.

Very soon, however, scientists began to see that Darwin was right. Other people followed suit and, even before Darwin died, the ideas that had once seemed so dangerous had become part of the nineteenth-century outlook.

The Origin of Species was not just a book about biology. It was a formula for revolution. And its painstaking, perfectionist author was one of the world's great revolutionaries.

Opposite: God creating the world, painted here by Raphael, an artist of the sixteenth century. According to the Christian Bible, the first man and the first woman were both directly created by God, as was each kind of animal. By Darwin's time, well-educated people did not believe the details of the Bible story quite as firmly as they once had done. But no one doubted that there was a special relationship between God and the humans He had created. Nor did they doubt that each animal species had been directly fashioned by God when He first created the world.

"The 'Darwinian Revolution' has always ranked alongside the 'Copernican Revolution' as one of those episodes in which a new scientific theory symbolizes a wholesale change in cultural values."
Peter J. Bowler, from "Evolution – the History of an Idea".

Above: Charles Darwin as a boy, with his younger sister Catherine. Their family thought she was much the brighter of the two. "I believe," Darwin remembered years later, "that I was in many ways a naughty boy."

"A disgrace to yourself"

He was also one of the unlikeliest. In his youth, no one thought he would add up to much. As his father once told him, in a fit of despair, "You care for nothing but shooting, dogs, and rat-catching, and you will be a disgrace to yourself and all your family." His school, which taught little but Latin and Greek, shared his father's disappointment.

Not that young Charles Darwin cared. Latin apart, he enjoyed his life in the prosperous country town of Shrewsbury in the heart of England. He grew up in a landscape full of gardens and hedgerows, with a great river running through it. When he could escape from school, he spent his time rambling through the woods. He loved collecting things like rocks and insects. He also loved dogs, plants, fishing, and his father, Robert: a mountain of a man who struck awe to the hearts of all who met him, his children included.

Wanted: a profession

Robert Darwin was a successful and highly-respected doctor. His wife, Susannah, was a member of the great family of Wedgwood pottery manufacturers. Charles, their fifth child and second son, was born in their red-brick mansion on February 12, 1809. With such a background, it was obvious he need never be short of money when he grew up. All the same, he was the son of a professional man. People felt he ought to follow *some* profession himself. The only question was: which?

Dr. Darwin decided that his rather stupid son might make a good doctor. At any rate, medicine was in the family, and Charles' elder brother, Erasmus, was already studying the subject at Edinburgh University. So, at the age of sixteen, Charles went off to Edinburgh.

Life there, he found, offered plenty of chances for doing the things he liked best. He collected sea creatures. He met other people who were interested in biology. He joined a natural history society; he wrote up his seashore findings, and read out what he'd written, to his new friends.

But, as for medicine, he hated it.

The lectures were even duller than Latin had

"I tried to make out the names of plants, and collected all sorts of things, shells, seals, franks, coins, and minerals. The passion for collecting which leads a man to be a systematic naturalist, a virtuoso, or a miser, was very strong in me, and was clearly innate."

Charles Darwin, describing himself at the age of eight.

Shrewsbury and the River Severn in 1800, not long before Darwin was born in a house overlooking the river. Although it was an important town, Shrewsbury at this date was still very rural. Darwin's earliest memory was of a cow running past his home's windows.

Top: The Wedgwoods' family medallion. The Wedgwoods were passionate opponents of the slave trade between Africa and the United States, which was then still legal. Even before he married Emma Wedgwood, Darwin fully shared their hatred of slavery, especially after seeing its results at first hand in South America.

Bottom: A beautiful piece of craftsmanship from the famous Wedgwood potteries.

been. Anatomy disgusted him; hospital case-work filled him with horror. Worst of all were the operations. In those days, operations were a nightmare: the screams, the blood, the agony.... Charles Darwin attended two of these dreadful sessions in the operating room. He never went a third time.

Young Mr. Darwin's horse-whip

Even to Dr. Darwin, it was plain that his son would not succeed in medicine. How about the Church? Good-naturedly, Charles agreed; it sounded quite a pleasant idea, being a country clergyman. But churchmen had to have degrees, so he had to go on studying for a while. He came south again, to Cambridge University, and plunged with gusto into a different sort of student life.

With his friends – a boisterous, hard-drinking, "horsey" set – he wined, dined, and played cards far into the night. By day, he attended to his two ruling passions, collecting beetles and shooting. He worked endlessly in his college room to improve his aim, firing blanks at a candle held by a patient friend. If the candle blew out, his aim had been accurate.

The noise bewildered the professors. "What an extraordinary thing it is," one said. "Mr. Darwin seems to spend hours in cracking a horse-whip in his room, for I often hear the crack when I pass under the windows."

Broadening horizons

Other professors were less puzzled by young Mr. Darwin's antics. Two were so impressed by his scientific interests that they became his friends. One was botanist, or plant specialist, John Henslow. Henslow broadened Darwin's horizons enormously. He took him on botany expeditions, welcomed him to his house, and urged him to read the books of the famous German explorer and naturalist, Alexander von Humboldt.

Crowded though his days were, Darwin still somehow managed to get his degree. In the summer of 1831, he went off with another professor, the geologist Adam Sedgwick, on a walking holiday in Wales, studying its rock formations and hunting for fossils. Then, on August 29, he came back home to Shrewsbury to find, waiting for him, a letter that changed his life.

The amazing invitation

In fact, there were two of them. One came from Darwin's friend Henslow. The other came from another Cambridge scientist, George Peacock. They contained an amazing invitation. The two men wanted Darwin to go on a voyage around the world.

The British Government, Peacock's letter explained, was doing a survey of the South American coast and some of the Pacific islands. He had

Darwin's Wedgwood grandparents and their children, at home on the family estate in Shropshire. Darwin's mother, who died while Darwin was a child, is on horseback in the middle of the painting, with her brother Josiah beside her. As Darwin's "Uncle Jos", the young horseman shown here would play a decisive part in helping to change the world.

been asked to recommend someone to act as the voyage's naturalist: observing, recording and collecting anything of interest in the lands the ship visited. He had passed this request on to Henslow.

Henslow's letter said that he had recommended Darwin.

The survey ship, *HMS Beagle,* would soon be leaving. Would Darwin be able to go with it?

The request took Darwin's breath away. He could scarcely believe it. Why did they want him, a mere beginner in the natural sciences? But Henslow had the answer to that too. The *Beagle's* captain was a young man, not much older than Darwin himself. He wanted company on the voyage: the company of a friend and equal. If he met Darwin and liked him, the search for a naturalist would be over.

Would Dr. Darwin consent?

Overwhelmed by his luck, Darwin was about to dash off his acceptance to Henslow. But he'd forgotten about his father. For years, Dr. Darwin had been trying to steer his wayward son into a worthwhile career. Now all his efforts were threatened by this hare-brained *Beagle* scheme. He refused to give his approval – unless one condition was met. "If," he told Charles, "you can find any man of common-sense who advises you to go I will give my consent."

All his life, Charles Darwin had been dominated by his father. Now, when everything hung on rebellion, he couldn't find it in himself to rebel. He didn't even think of it. Sadly, the young man wrote to Henslow with his refusal. Then he set off to visit his Wedgwood relations. The partridge-shooting season was about to start, and he didn't want to miss its opening days.

Uncle Josiah

He naturally told his uncle, Josiah Wedgwood, about the offer he'd had. And, to his joy, Uncle Jos reacted quite differently from his father. The *Beagle* trip, Uncle Jos said, was a splendid chance:

"It is intolerable to think of spending one's whole life like a neuter bee living all one's days solitarily in smoky, dirty London. Only picture to yourself a nice soft wife on a sofa, with good fire and books and music perhaps.... Marry, Marry, Marry!"

Charles Darwin.

a chance to be seized with both hands. He promptly dragged his nephew away from his shooting and, in a coach journey against the clock, bustled him back home.

Back in Shrewsbury, Dr. Darwin found himself faced both with his imploring son and his masterful brother-in-law. He had to admit it: Josiah *was* a "man of common-sense". He could not oppose Josiah's reasoning. He would consent to Charles taking his round-the-world voyage.

> *"The voyage of the Beagle has been by far the most important event in my life, and has determined my whole career; yet it depended on so small a circumstance as my uncle offering to drive me thirty miles to Shrewsbury."*
> Charles Darwin.

Meeting the captain ...

Within three days of getting the *Beagle* offer, Darwin was gleefully accepting the invitation. By September 5, he was in London, being interviewed by the *Beagle's* captain, Robert FitzRoy.

At first, FitzRoy didn't like him – because his nose was too small and snub! FitzRoy's own was long, curved and aristocratic, as befitted someone who had King Charles II in his ancestry. The captain had a theory that you could tell a man's character by his nose. And Darwin, he thought, had the nose of a weak man: not a good sign in someone signing on for a voyage of several years, around the world.

But, very quickly, Darwin's enthusiasm and good nature won the captain over completely. Everything was settled: the trip was on. It didn't matter that the ship's naturalist would not be getting any pay. Dr. Darwin would be meeting his son's expenses.

Instantly, the young man plunged into a frenzy of packing. He urged his family to send him his microscope and walking shoes. He ordered twelve new shirts and, on FitzRoy's advice, bought a rifle and pistols. Then he and the captain journeyed to Plymouth to see the *Beagle.*

Charles Darwin's microscope. Together with his notebook, his gun and his own observant eyes, it was one of the young naturalist's most important pieces of equipment. From his earliest years, Darwin was a scientist by instinct. He was passionately interested in the world as it was – not as other people's beliefs made it out to be. The microscope took him further and further into the mysteries of the real world.

... and meeting the *Beagle*

Even by the standards of the time, the *Beagle* was small. By today's she was tiny: no bigger than a coach from end to end. In this, over seventy people were to live, while their craft followed her long route through the oceans of the world.

19

Landsman that he was, Darwin was much impressed by the *Beagle*. He little dreamt of the agonies of sea-sickness that lay in wait for him within her wooden walls. He was, in fact, battling against sickness of another sort. The ship's departure was delayed; while waiting, Darwin noticed a rash had broken out on his hands. Aghast, he realized he had chest pains, too. Was there something wrong with his heart? He didn't dare go to a doctor. Suppose he was told he couldn't go on the voyage? But the pains grew no worse and at last, on December 27, 1831, the *Beagle* set off into the Atlantic Ocean. Charles was twenty-two years old: it would be five years before he would see England again.

Experiences of a lifetime

He had got there. He was in South America. After sixty-three days at sea, he was standing in a grove in a lush tropical forest. Looking around, Darwin felt delight flood through him.

Delight, he thought dazedly, was scarcely the word. He was in ecstasy.

All his life, he had been in love with the natural world: with birds and animals, with plants and the insects that fed on them. Now, he was in a paradise for birds, animals, insects, plants. They were all around him: darting, rustling, glistening, and filling the air with strange, provocative perfumes.

In a state close to worship, Darwin knew he was having the experience of a lifetime. The extraordinary thing was that it was followed by another ... and another. And a hundred more.

Darwin's first tropical forest was near Salvador, in the Brazilian region of Bahia. From there, he journeyed on down the Brazilian coast to Rio de Janeiro; then on again to Buenos Aires, to Tierra del Fuego and Cape Horn. As the *Beagle* came and went on her surveying tasks, Darwin would be put ashore for days – even weeks – to do his own job of observing and collecting. And, at every stop, there were moments of supreme feeling: joy, excitement, freedom.

Above: Safe anchorage: the "Beagle" during her voyage round the world, here pictured in Sydney, Australia. Darwin's quarters were at the stern, under the flag. His sleeping cabin was so small that he could only lie down if he pulled a drawer out of the locker at the end of his bed.

Left: Living conditions on a ship of Darwin's time, painted by the artist who accompanied the "Beagle", Augustus Earle.

21

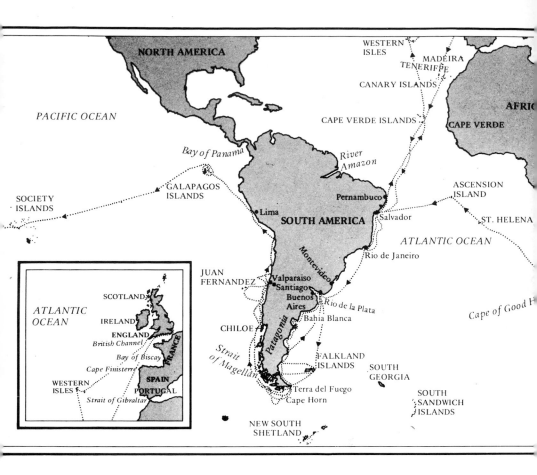

The map shows labels:

WESTERN ISLES · MADEIRA · TENERIFFE · CANARY ISLANDS · NORTH AMERICA · PACIFIC OCEAN · CAPE VERDE ISLANDS · CAPE VERDE · AFRIC · Bay of Panama · River Amazon · SOCIETY ISLANDS · GALAPAGOS ISLANDS · ASCENSION ISLAND · Lima · SOUTH AMERICA · Salvador · ST. HELENA · Pernambuco · ATLANTIC OCEAN · Montevideo · Rio de Janeiro · JUAN FERNANDEZ · Valparaiso · Santiago · Buenos Aires · Rio de la Plata · Cape of Good H · Bahia Blanca · CHILOE · Patagonia · FALKLAND ISLANDS · SOUTH GEORGIA · Strait of Magellan · Terra del Fuego · SOUTH SANDWICH ISLANDS · Cape Horn · NEW SOUTH SHETLAND

Inset map labels:

ATLANTIC OCEAN · SCOTLAND · IRELAND · ENGLAND · British Channel · Bay of Biscay · Cape Finisterre · WESTERN ISLES · FRANCE · SPAIN · PORTUGAL · Strait of Gibraltar

The "Beagle's" route on her great journey. She set sail from Britain at the end of 1831, and would not see the English Channel again until the latter part of 1836. As the map shows, the ship made several trips up and down the coasts of South America. It was while he was ashore during these trips that Darwin would make one of his most momentous discoveries: a graveyard of giant fossilized skeletons that belonged to species long extinct.

The man of action

All his life, Darwin had been an outdoor type: an energetic, sports-loving young man who enjoyed riding almost as much as shooting. In South America, he became a hardened man of action, tough and seemingly tireless.

In Montevideo, FitzRoy was asked to help put down a rebellion. Bristling with firearms, Darwin paraded the streets with the rest of the crew. While exploring on shore in Tierra del Fuego, FitzRoy and Darwin risked being stranded when a freak wave nearly washed their boat away. Darwin dashed forward and grabbed it before it vanished. When the *Beagle* returned north again, doubling back on her tracks, Darwin spent weeks in the saddle: riding

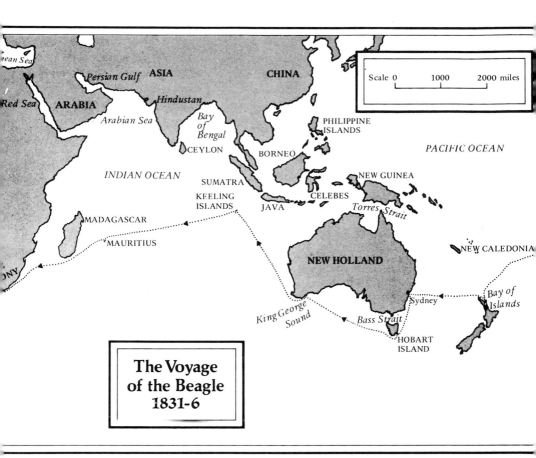

The map labels:

ean Sea
Persian Gulf · ASIA · CHINA
Red Sea · ARABIA · Hindustan
Arabian Sea · Bay of Bengal · PHILIPPINE ISLANDS
CEYLON · BORNEO · PACIFIC OCEAN
INDIAN OCEAN · SUMATRA · NEW GUINEA
KEELING ISLANDS · CELEBES
MADAGASCAR · JAVA · Torres Strait · NEW CALEDONIA
MAURITIUS · NEW HOLLAND
ONY · King George Sound · Sydney · Bay of Islands
Bass Strait
HOBART ISLAND

Scale 0 · 1000 · 2000 miles

The Voyage of the Beagle 1831-6

---

across the Argentinian Pampas, living off the land
and sleeping under the stars.

Preserving the evidence

Darwin's skill with his rifle made him a useful
member of any foraging party. But his main use
for it was to shoot specimens that, skinned and
stuffed, could be sent home to England. Pho-
tography, of course, had not been invented. The
best way to record a creature's appearance was to
kill one and preserve the body. Carefully, Darwin
packed up box after box to send back to Henslow:
stuffed mice, bags of seed, fish in pickling jars,
insects in nests of cotton wool.

Some of them did not travel well: Henslow once

complained that some of the mice were covered in fungus! But no decay could threaten another group of specimens that the ship's naturalist collected.

They had once been living tissue, but now they were made of stone. They were the fossilized skeletons of creatures that, thousands upon thousands of years ago, had browsed across Argentina's vast plains.

All the skeletons were enormous. Darwin had stumbled on a graveyard of the giants: "a catacomb," as he described it, "for monsters of extinct races."

The giants' graveyard

The giants' graveyard was a place called Punta Alta, close to the little Argentinian town of Bahia Blanca. The first bones Darwin dragged out had once belonged to a vast sloth-like creature, called Megatherium. Like a modern sloth, it fed on leaves. But it did not have to climb through branches to get them. It was easily big enough to sit on its hindquarters, reach up into a tree, and tear the branches down.

The next to emerge was another gigantic tree-

The hard-riding herdsmen, or guasos, of Chile, and their equally intrepid wives. Darwin got to know the guasos – and their Argentinian equivalents, the gauchos – very well. Of the two, he preferred the Argentinians, who were brilliant horsemen. The guasos seemed more interested in showing off the size of their huge spurs, as worn by the figure on the right.

browser, the Megalonyx. Then came a Sceli-dotherium, part-way between an anteater and an armadillo – and the size of a rhinoceros. Several more monsters of this type came out, to be followed by some remains that were truly baffling. One was a fossil horse: what *was* a horse doing in South America, so unimaginably long before the Spaniards introduced it in the 1500s? Another, the Toxodon, was a rodent the size of an elephant – a rodent that lived mainly in the water. It was like some vast, amazing cross between a rat and a hippo. It was like a gargantuan capybara, the modern world's biggest rodent.

Filled with excitement, Darwin had his huge finds hauled back to the *Beagle* where, to the de-spair of the crew, he stored them on the deck. In mixed fury and fun, the sailors moaned about the mess their "Philosopher" made of their tidy ship. Meanwhile, the "Philosopher" brooded intently over his precious horde. What was the link between the fossil creatures and their tiny modern equiv-alents? Why had these huge creatures died out? *How* had they died?

Why did they become extinct?

Devout Christians, he knew, had a reply to that. The cause was the great Flood: the Flood sent by God, so the Bible said, to punish the wicked world. During the Flood, nembers of most of the world's species had been rescued by Noah, in his Ark. These were the species that still continued to exist. But Megatherium and the rest had not been so lucky. Left outside, they were overwhelmed by the waters, and their species became extinct.

Darwin, the clergyman-to-be, knew his Bible as well as anyone. But the Flood theory now worried him. So did some other things about Christian teaching. After all, geologists were now saying that the earth was much, much older than Christian teaching maintained. Traditionally, churchmen taught that the world's history only went back a few thousand years. But, the scientists claimed, a few *million* years would be nearer the truth.

They were also saying that the world's surface

Evidence of life from the distant past, preserved in stone. Bones like these are only one sort of fossil. Another well-known type consists of a creature's outline impressed on stone, rather than of its actual remains. Fossils have been found that date from five hundred million years ago. Mammals only began to evolve about seventy million years ago so, compared to some fossil remains, Darwin's monsters did not date from very far back.

had been shaped, not in sudden floods sent by an angry God, but very slowly. Volcanoes, rivers, the sea with the litter of tell-tale shells it left behind: these were the things that ceaselessly changed the face of the earth. And changes were taking place, too, in the conditions in which the earth's animals and plants lived. Climates altered: places got hotter or colder, wetter or drier.

Perhaps, Darwin thought confusedly, it had been some change in living conditions that chased the giants out of existence. But what? Why should they all have died? And how did their smaller versions, the sloth, armadillo and the capybara, fit into the picture? In ancient times, did these poach on the giants' preserve, and eat up all their food?

The check on numbers

Something, at any rate, must have happened. After all, it happened all the time. *Something* set limits to the population of every species. Without it, the world would have been over-run and over-grown a million times over. Just how this check on population worked, Darwin wasn't sure. But he was absolutely certain it happened.

"I saw the spot where a cluster of fine trees once waved their branches on the shores of the Atlantic, when that ocean (now driven back 700 miles) came to the foot of the Andes.... I now beheld the bed of that ocean forming a chain of mountains more than 7000 feet in height."
Charles Darwin.

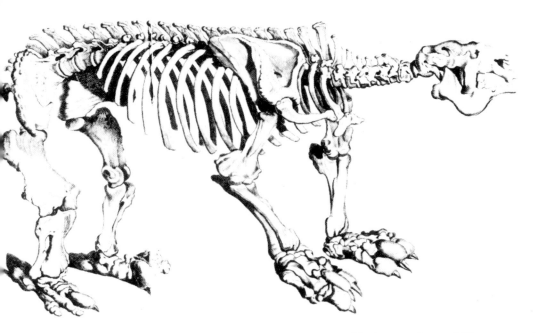

Sometimes, too, the check was over-severe, over-effective. The numbers of a plant or animal species started dropping. They got rarer and rarer. It was easy, Darwin reasoned, to work out the next stage. A rare species could easily become extinct. Was this what had happened to the monsters of the past?

It was logical; it made sense. It made more sense than stories of the Flood. But the Bible was still the Bible....

Thinking was easy. But matching thoughts up with beliefs was much, much harder.

The forces of nature

By the time the *Beagle* entered the Pacific Ocean, Darwin had abandoned his half-hearted plan of becoming a clergyman when he got home. He now knew what he was going to do with his working life. He would go on as he'd begun – as a naturalist.

Voyaging up the west coast of South America, he learned more and more about the forces of nature, and about what they could do. In the Andes, for example, he found beds of fossil shells, marooned at the top of a mountain. Anchored off the coast of Chile, he saw a volcano far in the

Myths – and a real-life monster. The amazing beings shown on the left appeared in a "scientific" book of 1553. They probably originated in adventurers' tales, repeated many times and grossly distorted on the way. The one-eyed woman and the wolf-headed man made a dramatic contrast with the Megatherium's fossil remains on the right, all sketched from life and meticulously numbered. By Darwin's time, scientists had made huge strides in their methods of observing and recording the world around them.

Above and opposite bottom: The present-day equivalents of the fossilized giants Darwin discovered near Bahia Blanca: the two-toed sloth (above), the capybara (bottom right) and the armadillo (bottom far right). The sloth's counterpart was the elephant-sized Megatherium. Darwin doubted whether any tree would have been strong enough to support the Megatherium.

distance, erupting in the night. It looked, he wrote, like a great star.

Soon after, at Concepcion, he witnessed the effects of a devastating earthquake. The 'quake had destroyed the town completely; before the Chileans' terrified eyes, it had even altered the shape of the land itself. Before it, they told Darwin, a group of offshore rocks had been below the water-line. And, some miles away, Captain FitzRoy found mussels hanging from rocks *well above* the high-water mark: another bed of marooned sea-shells in the making.

As always, Darwin observed, asked questions, made careful notes – and wondered about what he had seen. Meanwhile, the ship that carried him

Above: The South American ostrich, or Rhea.

Left: This Brazilian rainforest teems with the exotic life that so entranced Darwin. In spite of the destruction of the world's tropical rainforests, they still contain over half the world's known species of living things.

sailed on up the coast to Peru, then changed course for the north-west.

It was heading for the Equator, and for the Galapagos Islands.

The Galapagos

It was on September 15, 1835 that the *Beagle,* and twenty-six-year-old Charles Darwin, made landfall in the Galapagos Archipelago. Few people lived in this group of volcanic islands, but few ships passed by without stopping. Here, five hundred miles from the American mainland, sailors could collect and send off mail, re-fill their water barrels, and stock up with fresh meat. The meat came from the creatures that gave the islands their Spanish name: the *galapagos,* or giant tortoises, that paraded through the island scrub.

Darwin's first reaction to the islands was dismay. The scorching black shore, the parched shrubs and plants, the spiky cactus: they did not add up to an inviting prospect. But he sooned changed his mind. The *Beagle* cruised round the archipelago for a month, stopping at one island after another. And, daily, Darwin became more and more fascinated by what he saw. The islands, it seemed, bred mysteries as easily as they bred tortoises.

There was, for instance, the odd way in which the sea-lizards, or iguanas, behaved. The sea was their natural habitat – so why, if they were frightened, did they refuse to enter it? Several times, the naturalist hurled a squirming, flailing three-foot reptile into a rock pool. Each time, it swam straight back to shore. Could it be that the iguanas' only enemy were sharks? That might explain why they saw the shoreline's rocks as their best place of safety. It must be a sort of hereditary instinct, handed on from generation to generation.

The birds were fascinating, too. Darwin collected many different types of land-birds, half of them finches. Like so much else in the black lands, the male finches were usually black. But, in spite of this, there were big differences between them. One sort had a massive beak like a European hawfinch, powerful enough to open tough-shelled seeds. Another had the slender, pointed bill of an insect-eater. Others had beaks somewhere in between. And yet they were all finches, living in very similar conditions. Why should they look so different?

Different islands, different tortoises

The tortoises themselves were also creatures of mystery. The first riddle that they set Darwin was a small one, easily solved. At first, he could not work out who, on these desolate islands, made the well-marked paths that led away off the shore to the hills behind.

He soon learnt, however, that they were tortoise trails. For endless generations, the tortoises had trodden these broad tracks up to their regular drinking places, the springs in the middle of the island. That, in fact, was how the first visitors to the Galapagos had discovered the water there.

The second mystery would give Darwin – and many other people – far more trouble.

He was introduced to it by the vice-governor of the Galapagos, an Englishman named Nicholas Lawson. Most of the islands, as Darwin knew, had a tortoise population. One day, Lawson casually said that he could tell at a glance which island any captured tortoise had come from. Other islanders said they could do the same. Tortoises from different islands had different markings, different shapes, even different tastes. The tortoises from James Island, in the middle of the group, were famous for tasting especially good.

What was the explanation?

At first, Darwin did not pay much attention to this local gossip. Then, with a jolt, he realized its importance. It must have been a nasty moment. He had already collected specimens from two of the Galapagos islands – and he had muddled the two sets up.

All the same, he knew the islanders were right. And he also knew he was on the track of something

The findings ... and the evidence, here laid out beside the island each bird is from. For many years, people believed that Darwin's thoughts on evolution had been sparked off by the Galapagos finches and their widely-differing beaks. In fact, it was the islands' thrushes and tortoises that first caught his attention. Only after his return did he find out that among his meticulous scientific records he had collected thirteen different finch species.

Right: As dark as the rocks they bask on, the sea iguanas of the present-day Galapagos Islands display the short, broad heads and strong claws that Darwin noted on his visit 150 years ago. A large one, he recalled, weighed nine kilograms. So his experiment to check on their shore-seeking instincts must have been hard work!

Opposite: A Galapagos land iguana, and a giant tortoise. Darwin found sea-going iguanas throughout the islands, but the brown land version shown here occurred only on the islands in the middle of the group. "When we were left at James Island," Darwin recalled in his "Journal", "we could not for some time find a spot free from their burrows on which to pitch our single tent."

very odd indeed. The islands were very similar; they had similar climates; most of them were even in sight of each other. And, yet, each seemed to have its own special population of creatures.

Several islands, he was sure, had their own special type of tortoise. Did they also have their own special type of finch? It was hard to tell; again, Darwin cursed the way he had mixed his specimens up. But it seemed possible. And then there were the island thrushes, or mockingbirds. There were some odd differences about them, too.

How had these differences come about? *Why* had they come about? Had all the different tortoises and thrushes really been created by God, each sort for its own little island? Or was there some other

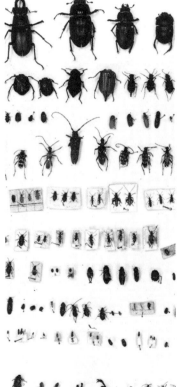

explanation – an explanation that overturned everything people believed about life on earth?

As, on October 20, 1835 the *Beagle* sailed away from the islands for good, she took with her one very thoughtful, very puzzled ship's naturalist.

Recognition – and hard work

After a voyage that took him over the Pacific, across the Indian Ocean, and northward up through the Atlantic, Charles Darwin, aged twenty-seven, returned home to England in October, 1836. To his surprised delight, he found people had already heard of him and his work.

Other scientists beside Henslow had read the letters he had sent back to Cambridge with the carefully-packed boxes. Now they wanted to meet him. The great geologist, Charles Lyell, invited him to dinner. The prestigious Geological Society admitted him to their ranks. Soon he was made the society's secretary. On top of this, he had all his own scientific affairs to see to.

Later, Darwin would remember the two years after his return as the busiest of his life. The *Beagle's* voyage might be over, but his work as its naturalist was scarcely half-done. He now had to go through all the specimens he'd collected: examining them, classifying them, recording the results. His first reaction to this task was paralyzed despair. But, with the help of other scientific experts, it turned out easier than he feared.

He also had a great deal of writing to do. He edited the five-volume set of books describing the voyage's zoological work. He also wrote a book of his own: his journal of the voyage. It was to form a companion volume to two others, written by FitzRoy and by the *Beagle's* earlier captain.

Darwin rebels

It was impossible to carry out all his work from his home in Shrewsbury. So, in 1837, Darwin took rooms in Great Marlborough Street in central London. He enjoyed all the scientific and social life London had to offer. But he soon discovered he hated the city itself. It was grubby, it was smelly, it was shut-in. And he couldn't escape: he had far too much work to do.

After a few months of this, Darwin rebelled. His life was becoming as dry and dusty as Great Marlborough Street itself. He had to do something. He couldn't leave London, but he could do something even better. He could get married! He began to look for a wife and, the next year, he found her. He did not have far to look: she was his first cousin, Emma Wedgwood, youngest daughter of Uncle Jos. They got married in 1839 on January 29, shortly before Darwin's thirtieth birthday. It was the year in which his *Journal of Researches* of the *Beagle's* voyage appeared. Both the book and the marriage were to be glorious successes.

Something is wrong

Emma Darwin came from a big, sociable family. Naturally, she soon started making a sociable home for her new husband. People like Henslow and Lyell were regular visitors.

As a young man, Darwin had glowed with health and fizzed with high spirits. During the *Beagle* voyage, he'd thrived on the energetic demands. Now, back in England, he was living a much easier life. He was famous, he was happily married, and he had a brilliant future in front of him. But, all the same, something was wrong in his life. What was it? He was fast becoming an invalid – and no one could work out why.

The Darwins leave London

He felt tired, giddy, sick. The tiniest effort or excitement left him weak with exhaustion. Even chatting to friends wore him out. Obviously, he could not go on leading an active life in London. More than anything else, he needed peace and quiet.

In 1842, Charles, aged thirty-three, and Emma left London, and moved to the village of Downe in south-east England. Their new home was called Down House. Here, Darwin would live for the rest

Emma Darwin, shortly after her marriage. The dinner-parties she gave for her husband included one for the Henslows and Lyells that she made famous in a letter to her sister. The distinguished scientists were as bad at social chat as their wives were skilled. In spite of everything, the party went off well – but, after it, Darwin was in a state of near-collapse.

of his life: engrossed in his work and seeing few people except his family and closest friends.

What was the matter with him?

Many people have tried to work out what was the matter with Darwin. One theory is that he had Chagas's disease, an illness carried by the notorious Benchuga bug of South America. Darwin had been bitten by a Benchuga in the Andes.

Or perhaps the trouble lay, not in his body, but in his feelings. He'd suffered once already from obvious "nerves": in Plymouth as, impatient and keyed-up, he waited for the *Beagle* to set sail. Then, his tightly-stretched emotions had expressed themselves through chest pains and a rash. Now, he had a far, far more difficult problem to handle.

He was going to tear the world apart: his own, and everyone else's.

By the time of his marriage, Darwin had already started on the work that would one day make him world-famous. And he knew, even then, that his ideas might wreck his life. If they were right, for example, they would break his devout wife's heart. Everyone he respected would criticize him, blame him, loathe him. How could he stand up to it all: he, Darwin, who all his life had tried to be pleasant to everybody?

And yet, as a scientist, he couldn't stop himself trying to work out the truth.

The evidence of the birds

It all started with the Galapagos mockingbirds: the frail little corpses that had been sent back to England with the rest of Darwin's specimens. Among the specialists that worked on Darwin's collection was the Zoological Society's ornithologist, John Gould. In 1837, after examining the Galapagos birds, Gould told Darwin that they really did include several different sorts of thrush. And they were not merely different varieties, as Darwin himself had thought. Varieties could breed with each other, to produce hybrids, but the Galapagos thrushes

Its natural habitat: a heavy-beaked finch investigates a Galapagos cactus for food. The thirteen finch species on the islands evolved from their single parental species because the Galapagos offered a wide variety of uncontested foodstuffs and nesting-places. Unthreatened by rival species, the finches began to adapt to fill these vacant "ecological niches".

could not have done that. They belonged to three separate species.

As for the finches, Gould's report was even more staggering. Darwin had collected no less than *thirteen* different species.

So many differences!

Alas, the finch specimens had been muddled together. With the thrushes, though, there was no question. The three different species had come from three different islands – one species to each island. Three species of thrush; thirteen species of finch … and then there were the tortoises, too. It was enough to make the head spin.

So many differences: so many variations on a basic theme. It was obvious enough, Darwin thought, that the theme was a South American one. To begin with, the Galapagos creatures must have been blown, or carried, or transported in some other way, across the sea from the South American mainland.

And then, when they arrived in the islands: ah, that was the real mystery. Did the South American

Extremes in beak formation, illustrated by the seed-eating finch on the left and the delicately-billed "warbler finch" on the right. Warblers can survive with delicate beaks because they live on insects and fruit. The giant tortoises of the Galapagos are even more varied. There are no less than fourteen different types. Some are unique to a single island, and some share the largest island with others. Each one of these island-sharers, however, occupies a separate volcanic area from the other types.

creatures start changing – evolving – into new species? New, different species for each island: for each little world on its own, cut off from the rest by the surrounding sea?

Many of the islands, of course, were quite close to each other but, streaming through the whole group from east to west, there ran a series of strong sea-currents. These westerly currents cut off the southern islands from the northern ones, while James Island – the source of the best tortoise-meat in the whole group – was isolated twice over. Between James and the bigger island of Albemarle, another current poured northward.

Then there were the winds; or rather, the lack of winds. Darwin remembered the strange, stifling atmosphere of the black lands. No gales blew to carry helpless birds or insects from one island to the next. Once a species somehow got a foothold on one of the Enchanted Isles, there its members stayed ... and began to change.

It made sense. It made a lot more sense than the idea that God had specially made different creatures for each of these remote specks in the Pacific.

Time and time again, Darwin wondered *just* how it happened; why it happened. Within a few weeks, he had become obsessed. In July 1837, he set aside a special notebook for recording anything else he could find out about such changes and variations, anywhere in the world.

Charles Darwin had joined the evolutionists.

"It is impossible to reflect on the changed state of the American continent without the deepest astonishment. Formerly it must have swarmed with great monsters: now we find mere pygmies, compared with the antecedent, allied races."
Charles Darwin.

Lamarck's giraffe

Evolution was not a completely new idea. Men of science had already begun to question the idea that all species – living and extinct – were individually created by God, in the forms that they still wore. One of the people who questioned the "creationist" theory was Darwin's own famous grandfather, a doctor and thinker named Erasmus Darwin. Another was a French naturalist, the Chevalier de Lamarck.

In the early 1800s Lamarck had declared that all the world's species, humans included, had emerged

– or evolved – from other, earlier species. The process took place, he argued, because living things all tried to adapt themselves as well as possible to their living conditions. This, for example, was how giraffes got their long necks. They were descended from hungry, shorter-necked animals who had stretched high into trees for food.

A lifetime's stretching, said Lamarck, made their necks grow. And the young of the "neck-stretchers" would also have long necks!

The holes in Lamarck's argument are now obvious. Today, we can see that he had got the situation back to front. The earliest long-necked creatures certainly passed their shape on to their offspring – but they themselves had been born with long necks, too. It was *because* their necks happened to be longer than average for their species that they could reach into trees for extra food. And, because they could get more food than shorter-necked animals, they tended to live longer. They lived long enough to give birth to long-necked young like themselves.

In its time, however, Lamarck's argument was an intellectual breakthrough. He made a mistake over the way evolution works. But, by boldly stating that evolution itself took place, he provoked other scientists into thinking and arguing about it.

The arguments, naturally, came thick and fast, and the evolutionists had a hard time. Lamarck's views were demolished by the leading French naturalist of the day, Baron Georges Cuvier, a fanatical creationist. A few other people explored the idea, but they did not make much headway.

It was at this point that Darwin came on the scene with the first of his "species notebooks"

The great project starts

His research was to be basically very simple. At first, he rejected the idea of trying to prove or disprove a pre-conceived theory. Instead, he planned to do the opposite. He was just going to collect facts about the differences between living things: all and any facts, as many as he possibly could, drawn from as many sources as he could contact. And he would

The work that Darwin did on a whole variety of species was very detailed and precise. He carefully observed and noted all his discoveries for over forty years. This scientific drawing of a beetle is one of the many records he kept – and which led to his amazing discovery.

While working on his theory of evolution, Darwin took up pigeon-keeping. In the "Origin", he noted that most pigeons had about twelve tail feathers. But fantails, like the one shown here, had thirty or even forty. So, had the fantail emerged from a completely different (and now lost) wild pigeon species? Or had it been created from the wild rock-pigeon – along with all the other fancy pigeon breeds? After breeding fantails that had rock-pigeon markings, Darwin decided that the second answer was the right one.

then see what they added up to.

So, as Great Marlborough Street got hotter and dustier by the day, Darwin started his great project. When he could spare time from his *Beagle* work, he talked to animal breeders and gardeners. He sent off questionnaires to scientists. He read enormously. Later, after marrying and moving to Down House, he observed and experimented tirelessly: watching his collection of pigeons, studying the pollination of the Down holly-trees, crossing cabbage varieties and analyzing the results.

The struggle for existence

By this time, however, Darwin had a theory to work around – something to test his findings against; something to re-shape and then test again. In 1838, he happened to read a book by an influential British economist, Thomas Malthus. Called *An Essay on the Principle of Population,* it painted a grim future for the human race. Malthus calculated that, left completely to their own devices, human populations increased very quickly. They doubled every twenty-five years. Food supplies could never increase so fast, so humans were constantly threatened by starvation. The only things that kept populations under control were disasters like war, famine and disease. If some people were to live, others had to die. Existence itself was a constant struggle.

Every twenty-five years! The phrase echoed around Darwin's brain like a burst of gunfire. And Malthus was only talking about people. How about animals and plants? They sometimes doubled their populations in days rather than years. All of them were faced with a savage competition for what nourishment was available. There was not – there never could be – enough food to go around. Many living things perished: the "check" he had observed earlier came into operation. But others survived.

And who were these survivors? They were the creatures and plants that were best-suited to their circumstances. They were the ones who were just a little different from the rest; the ones who were better-equipped to win the competition. And, winning

it, they would survive to breed; their offspring, too, and their offspring's offspring....

Darwin's theory

A lot of time would go by before Darwin was able to propose his great theory of evolution in its final form. But, only two years after returning to Britain, he had already worked out its central idea: an idea that, today, sounds so obvious, so simple.

Even as finally published, the theory's basic message was still a very simple one. Evolution, it said, *did* take place. The world's species had not been shaped in one single burst of divine creation. Instead, they had developed – evolved – from species that had existed earlier.

The force that made new species evolve, Darwin said, was natural selection: the process that ensured

The survival of species, as interpreted by the Christian Bible. As the Great Flood threatens the world, Noah loads breeding pairs of the world's creatures into the Ark, here painted by an artist of the 1600s. Anything that did not enter the Ark became extinct as soon as the Flood covered the earth. People who held this view, like the "Beagle's" Captain FitzRoy, were horrified by Darwin's theory of the "survival of the fittest".

the preservation of any features that specially helped an individual to survive. Within a species, these special features would tend to be handed on from one generation of survivors to another. In the end, they would be shared by a huge number of individuals. These would now all be members of a new species, that was different from the one it had sprung from.

From the new species, one or more even newer species could spring. They, in turn, could parent many more. And, as time went by, the newcomer species would vary more and more widely both from each other and from their original parent species.

"Confessing a murder"

Darwin spent about fourteen years working on his theory: testing it, spotting likely objections, working out ways of answering them. In 1842, he jotted down a rough outline in pencil of his views. He wrote a longer version in 1844, when he was thirty-five. He knew only too well that he was playing with fire. Around this time, he confessed to a friend that he thought species *did* change over time; it was, he said, "like confessing a murder."

This was why he took such trouble with his research. He'd realized there was only one way of getting such dangerous ideas accepted. Each step in the argument had to be backed up with hard, solid evidence: evidence that the most fanatical of creationists could not deny.

Daily life

Soon after his "confession", he took a break – an eight-year break – from evolution, and studied barnacles instead. He emerged from this a fully-trained biologist, something that helped enormously when he returned to his species work.

His health, though, did not allow him to work more than a few hours a day. The rest of the time, he read, walked, wrote innumerable letters, played backgammon with Emma. (He always kept a note of the score: his records show that he was a better player than his wife – but only by a tight margin!)

His working routine seldom changed. He'd get up early and, rain or shine, take a before-breakfast stroll in the garden. Breakfast was at 7:45; he then went straight into his study to work until 9:30: the best working time of the day, he always said. Then, the mail arrived; he took a break until 10:30, and worked again until about noon. Noon really marked the end of his working day; feeling satisfied, Darwin would call to one of his beloved dogs and take another walk.

His route usually led him to the little wood he and Emma had created in a far corner of the grounds. Part of it was made up of big old oaks that had been growing there for hundreds of years. To this, he had added lime trees, hazels and hollies, while Emma had planted flowering shrubs. All around it ran a path, covered with sand dug from a pit within the wood itself. The family called it the "Sand-walk". Darwin loved it, and his children made it their special playground.

He adored his children; they adored him in return. He spent a lot of time with them. When they were ill, he'd turn his study into a sickroom: the patient would curl up on a sofa while the great scientist

"I seem to remember him gently touching a flower he delighted in; it was the same simple admiration that a child might have."
Francis Darwin, writing about his father, Charles.

Home life at Down. Sitting in the window, Emma Darwin reads aloud to some of her teenage children. The dog in the foreground, named Bob, became famous when Darwin described him in his book, "The Expression of the Emotions in Man and Animals". Bob hated it when his master made a detour on his midday walk to look at his greenhouses. "His look of dejection," Darwin wrote, "was known to every member of the family, and was called his 'hot-house face'."

When the squirrel (left) was introduced into Britain last century, it began to compete with the native red squirrel (right) for food and living space. Since it is bigger than its rival – and also can eat a more varied diet – it is now much more common than the red species it has ousted. Its victory illustrates a point Darwin made almost twenty years before: the struggle for survival was much more severe when it occurred between closely-related species.

worked alongside. When they were well, he let them help with his research, following bees around the garden to plot their regular routes. All the same, they still thought their father worked *too* hard: one of them, aged four, even tried bribing him to come out and play!

His days went on and on, a placid mixture of methodical work and happy, comfortable family life. Darwin had plenty of money, left to him by his father. He had no need to earn any. He had no need to do anything he didn't want to: like putting forward his life's work – his species theory – to be judged, criticized, attacked.

In 1858, Alfred Russel Wallace's letter from the East Indies came crashing into this peaceful setting like a thunderbolt.

Darwin's friends

It could not have come at a worse time. While Darwin was agonizing over what to do, scarlet fever – then a very dangerous disease – had appeared in the village. Within days, it reached the nursery at Down House. Within a few days more, it killed the Darwins' youngest son.

For a short while, the scientist was quite crushed by the twin tragedies that had overwhelmed him. But he was helped through them by devoted friends like Charles Lyell and the botanist, Sir Joseph Hooker, who was assistant-director of the Royal Botanic Gardens at Kew.

Lyell and Hooker calmed Darwin's anguished conscience, stopped him giving his priority away to Wallace, and arranged for the joint Darwin-Wallace reading to the Linnean Society of London. The scientists who heard it were interested, but cautious. They did not want to cross swords with the powerful Lyell and Hooker!

From Darwin's point of view, the sky at least hadn't fallen in. Encouraged by his friends, he decided that there was now no help for it: he had to publish something on this theory as soon as possible. And, on a visit to the Isle of Wight, he started writing his "book of the book", *The Origin of Species:* "When on board *HMS Beagle*, as naturalist, I was much struck with certain facts …"

Where did humans fit in?

By Darwin's own standards – and by those of the nineteenth century – the *Origin* was a fairly short book. But it still ran to over six hundred pages of argument and evidence. On the last page but two came one of the most important sentences of all. Acceptance of his views, Darwin said, would cause a revolution in the study of natural history. New fields of research would be opened up. And "much light will be thrown on the origin of man and his history."

In all those six hundred pages, this is almost the only mention of the human race that Darwin allowed himself. And it is clear what he was trying to do. He had his own definite views on the origin of the human species, and they were even *more* controversial than the rest of his ideas. But, with that covering sentence in the *Origin*, he was trying to say that he hadn't – yet – worked out how humans fitted into his theory.

Even at the time he cannot really have expected to fool anyone. For what, only five pages earlier,

This blue-eyed white cat looks alert to every sound caught by its big ears. But how much can it really hear? Writing in the 1850s, Darwin observed that "cats which are entirely white and have blue eyes are generally deaf". Cat breeders still face this problem today, and are advised not to breed from deaf, blue-eyed whites. Deaf female cats do not make good parents, as they cannot hear their kittens calling out. In the wild, this would mean that the kittens would probably not survive. Natural selection would abolish the deafness factor.

45

had he written? "I believe," a crucial passage ran, "that animals are descended from at most only four or five progenitors, and plants from an equal or lesser number." It was followed, more tentatively, by the suggestion that all plants and animals might be descended from one *single* ancestral form.

And what, from any rational point of view, was man if not ... an animal?

Publication day

Under its full title – *On the Origin of Species by Means of Natural Selection, or the Preservation of Favoured Races in the Struggle for Life* – Charles Darwin's book was published in London on November 24, 1859. The publishers, John Murray, printed 1,250 copies.

Darwin worried that Murray would be left with unsold stock, but he was wrong. Before the day was out, British book-sellers had placed an order for every copy. They thought they might have a best-seller on their hands.

They were right. But it was to be far, far more than that.

A monkey for a grandmother?

With a smile, the bishop glanced at the scientist. Suddenly hard-eyed, the scientist stared back at the bishop. All around, the big Oxford hall went very quiet. Just for a second, no one coughed, no one rustled papers. The ladies in their big crinolines, packed tightly into seats by the windows, stopped flicking their fans.

And, in the hot, breathless silence, one sentence still hummed in the air like an echo. Its words were courteous, formal, even witty. But they dripped with venom.

Was it, the bishop had asked the scientist, on his grandfather's side or his grandmother's that he was descended from a monkey?

Suddenly, the tension broke. Wild applause broke out as Samuel Wilberforce, Bishop of Oxford, sat down. Wilberforce looked around happily; yes,

"Can we doubt (remembering that many more individuals are born than can possibly survive) that individuals having any advantage, however slight, over others, would have the best chance of surviving and of procreating their kinds? On the other hand, we may feel sure that any variation in the least degree injurious would be rigidly destroyed."

Charles Darwin, from "The Origin of Species".

his speech had really gone very well. That should put an end to this wild theory of Mr. Darwin's. Of course, he hadn't known much about the Darwin business himself – but that didn't matter. One of his side had briefed him, and oratory had done the rest. Not for nothing was he nicknamed "Soapy Sam". And the bishop smiled even more broadly.

He did not notice it when, with an air of triumph, the scientist slapped himself on the knee. Thomas Henry Huxley, a leading biologist and a Darwin supporter, had thought of the right reply.

The downfall of "Soapy Sam"

All around the hall, there were calls for Professor Huxley to speak. Professor Henslow, in the chair, nodded to his fellow-scientist, and Huxley stood up. Gleefully, the 1860 meeting of the British Association for the Advancement of Science brought itself to order.

Its members had been promised a discussion of

Descended from monkeys? Middle-class Victorians worshipped the idea of the perfect lady. She was the "angel in the house", the protector of morals, and the source of everything beautiful in domestic life. As shown by this cartoon of the 1860s, the idea of her link with wild, hairy apes was totally unthinkable. Most people did not realize they had got the idea wrong in any case.

Samuel Wilberforce, also known as "Soapy Sam"; in a review of the "Origin", he wrote:

"Man's derived supremacy over the earth; man's power of articulate speech; man's gift of reason; man's freewill and responsibility ... are ... irreconcilable with the degrading notion of the brute origin of him who was created in the image of God."

Darwin's controversial theory. They were getting something much more sensational.

Huxley, unlike Wilberforce, was a quiet, plain speaker. And his speech began quietly. He defended Darwin; he explained what Darwin's theory meant; he cast doubts on the bishop's grasp of science. And then, abruptly, he closed in for the kill.

Suppose that the bishop was right: suppose that he – Huxley – was descended from a monkey. What of it? He would rather be descended from an ape, he declared firmly, than from a man who "used great gifts to obscure the truth."

Or, in other words, from such a cultured, honey-tongued spreader of mischief and error as ... the bishop himself.

"During the voyage of the Beagle I had been deeply impressed by discovering ... great fossil animals covered with armour like that on the existing armadillos; secondly, by the manner in which closely allied animals replace one another in proceeding southwards over the Continent.... It was evident that such facts as these, as well as many others, could only be explained on the supposition that species gradually became modified; and the subject haunted me. But it was equally evident that neither the action of the surrounding conditions, nor the will of the organisms (especially in the case of plants) could account for the innumerable cases in which organisms of every kind are beautifully adapted to their habits of life...."

Charles Darwin, on how he started his work on 'The Origin of Species'. It was observations like this that inflamed the bishop and led to furious debates and disagreements.

Pandemonium breaks out

Instantly, there was pandemonium. There were cheers, boos, shrieks of laughter, and tumultuous clapping. Down the platform from the triumphant Huxley, Darwin's friend Hooker relaxed. "Soapy Sam" sat silent and mortified. A group of other clergymen protested furiously. Further back in the hall, the students of Oxford whooped and yelled with delight. Over by the windows, there was another sensation; sagging like a collapsing tent, a fashionable lady had fainted with shock.

And what was this? In the thick of the audience, a man had leapt to his feet, yelling and holding high a Bible. Here, he shouted, was the source of all truth: here and here alone. Robert FitzRoy – by now fifty-four, a vice-admiral, a religious zealot and still an ardent creationist – had returned from the past, like a ghost, to haunt the present. Five years later, he would commit suicide.

"Darwin's bulldog" needs his teeth

By the end of the meeting, it was plain that Darwin's side had won. It didn't matter that Darwin himself was absent. (He was too ill to come.) In people like Huxley and Hooker, he had found champions who could defend him much better than he could defend himself.

Huxley was, in fact, a new arrival in the Darwin camp. He'd been asked to review *The Origin of Species* for Britain's leading paper, *The Times*. And he'd praised it warmly. This was a great piece of luck for both Darwin and his theory. From then on, Huxley would spring to their defence whenever needed, and was soon known as "Darwin's bulldog".

As the Oxford meeting showed, the bulldog needed all his teeth. Darwinism – as it was called – had some formidable enemies. They fell into two main camps, the scientific and the religious.

The scientists' group attacked Darwin on several different grounds. Some scientists objected to his working methods. All he'd done, they said, was prove what he *wanted* to prove, a notoriously easy

"Darwin's bulldog": leading biologist Thomas Henry Huxley brought the meeting to a climax by vanquishing Bishop Wilberforce. Huxley summed up his view of the "Origin" much more simply than the Bishop. "My reflection," he once wrote, "when I first made myself master of the central idea … was, 'How extremely stupid not to have thought of that!'."

task. Others objected to the time-scale Darwin suggested for the history of evolution. No scientist believed that the world was only four thousand years old. But three hundred million years, Darwin's figure, seemed too big a leap in the other direction. (In fact, it is a colossal under-estimate.)

Then there were a string of queries about the way heredity actually worked. Just how did the fastest, strongest or most adaptable creatures hand their special gifts on to their offspring? No one, Darwin included, could guess that the answers to this were already emerging – and they would fit in with Darwin's theory. In a monastery garden in Central Europe, a Czech named Gregor Mendel was crossing varieties of garden pea and studying the results. His work would make him the father of the science of genetics.

The lords of creation deposed

Unlike the scientific objections, the religious ones tended to cluster around one issue. Everyone saw through Darwin's attempt to keep humans out of his theory. It was obvious that, if his law of natural selection worked, it worked for humans as well.

This meant that they were not "made in God's image". They were not the lords of creation, the superiors of everything else in the world. They were living creatures like any other, evolved from earlier living creatures.

Arguments like these directly threatened the Christian church's authority. Until then, Christians had believed what the Bible told them. If the Bible was proved wrong, their religion was a useless sham. Christian doctrines did not make sense – and there was something even worse.

What really horrified people was the way that Darwin seemed to link the semi-divine human race with monkeys: with smelly, hairy, monkeys, famous for their pranks and the wild way they behaved. In fact, everyone had put two and two together to make five. Nowhere did Darwin say that humans were descended from the great apes. But the idea stuck. People made monkey jokes and sang monkey songs. Magazines printed monkey cartoons.

Brothers under the skin? To cartoonists, the confusion that surrounded Darwin's views on humanity's origins was a gift in a million. What Darwin himself really thought on the subject was rather different. "*Our* ancester," he once wrote to Charles Lyell, "was an animal which breathed water, had a swim bladder, a great swimming tail, an imperfect skull, and undoubtedly was a hermaphrodite!"

Evolution at work, here shown in an artist's reconstruction. This crow-like "bird" preening its wing is an Archaeopteryx. Like a reptile, it has scales, a long tail and teeth. But its tail is clothed in feathers, while its wings look almost like those used by a bird today. It lived over 130 million years ago.

Darwinism meets a need

To begin with, the Darwinists must sometimes have wondered if they would ever win the day. They were facing the combined might of the Church and most of the scientific world. And many people seemed to have misunderstood Darwin's theory anyway.

The Darwin supporters never managed to demolish all the religious opposition. But, with their fellow-scientists, they had far more success. And this victory came surprisingly fast.

Was Darwinism, then, an idea that was already "in the air"? Darwin himself didn't really agree. However, the time was certainly right for something that explained so much that was otherwise inexplicable. His theory met a need that biologists hadn't quite realized they possessed.

What they needed was a scientific method of thinking about the origin of species: a method that dealt in facts, measurements, proofs. All they'd had was a religious method of thinking; a method that dealt in beliefs, feelings and facts that could not be proved.

Evolution, as explained by Darwin, gave them the scientific way of thinking that they needed.

The evidence of the fossils

Many scientists didn't agree with all of Darwin's theory. In particular, the idea of natural selection worried them a lot. But it helped that Darwin did not say this was the *only* force that powered evolution: just the main one. It also helped that, in 1861, fossils were discovered in Germany that proved Darwin right on one point: the evolutionary link between reptiles and birds. The German fossils were the remains of an archaeopteryx. It had a reptile's bones, a reptile's tail ... and feathers.

What helped most of all was the part played by "Darwin's bulldog" and his helpers. Huxley and the others were already influential men, and they became more influential still. Naturally, they used their influence to make sure that university jobs went to young, up-and-coming Darwinists!

By 1870 something like three-quarters of Britain's biologists had become evolutionists as well. In the 1880s, scientists who did not support Darwin's views were the exception rather than the rule. Darwinism took root in the United States as well, and in parts of Europe. And in Japan – then just emerging from a feudal past of shoguns and samurai – modern thinkers read translations of Darwin and agreed with them.

The unbelievable had happened. Charles Darwin had won.

The evidence of the fossils. The remains of the Archaeopteryx, preserved in stone for millions of years, and discovered soon after the "Origin" was published. The fossil clearly shows both the Archaeopteryx's reptilian features, such as its tail and clawed wings, and the imprint of its feathers.

Darwin takes a back seat

For years, Darwin had been dreading the controversy that he knew his work would cause. But, when the storm came, he coped with it surprisingly well. Sensibly, he never let himself be drawn into open warfare: he left that to Huxley and the others. His friends' support gave him the confidence to bear criticism. He was even able to laugh at "Soapy Sam's" barbed jokes.

His daily life continued just as before. The scientists argued, the churchmen trumpeted, and the energetic Huxley fought battles in front of and behind the scenes. But, at Down House, the scientist who had started it all went on with his normal routine of work, walks, rests and listening to Emma's piano. Darwin was by now in his fifties.

Although his working hours were so short, he got through a great deal. First, there was a lot to do on *The Origin* itself. It went into six separate editions; in his usual painstaking way, he kept altering and correcting them. Then there was all his new work, to be written up as books or scientific papers. And then there was the stream of articles he wrote for magazines, on subjects ranging from chemistry to hedgehogs.

Naturally, evolution and the force that powered it ran like a linking thread through most of what he did. The next book after *The Origin*, for instance, looked at the effect evolution had had on the way orchids were pollinated. A paper on climbing plants showed how their tendrils helped their chances of survival.

The origins of the human species

Darwin went on to a subject that was more daunting still. It was the one he had dodged in *The Origin*. In 1867, aged fifty-eight, he started writing a book on the origin of the human species.

The result, called *The Descent of Man*, was published in 1871. In it, Darwin plunged boldly into describing the links – the taboo links – that bound human beings to the animal world, and especially to the apes.

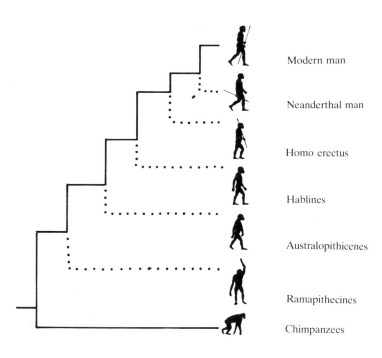

Modern man

Neanderthal man

Homo erectus

Hablines

Australopithicenes

Ramapithecines

Chimpanzees

Humans and apes had similar bodies and sense organs. They caught some of the same diseases. The human embryo developed in a similar way to the ape embryo: both, for a while, had tails, but this reminder of a four-footed ancestor had vanished by the time they were born. Nor did the similarities stop there. Humans and animals experienced similar emotions, such as happiness and boredom. And the human race's greatest asset, intelligence, was also, to a lesser extent, found in animals.

None of this, of course, meant that humans were actually descended from apes. What it did mean was that, back in the past, humans and apes had evolved from the same ancestral species: a four-footed one, at that.

Here it was at last, backed with a mass of convincing detail: the notorious Charles Darwin's answer to the story of Adam and Eve. As Darwin expected, it caused a sensation. Churchmen deplored it, reviewers attacked it, and the book-reading public rushed to buy it.

Related, yes; descended from each other, no. In their early, horrified, reaction to Darwin's work, most Victorians made the mistake of drawing a line directly linking the ape at the bottom and the modern man, or "Homo sapiens" at the top. Darwin himself was actually saying something quite different. Today, the ancestor that man and the apes have in common is believed to have been something like a tree shrew!

The twilight years. In this famous painting, Emma Darwin – who was a gifted pianist – plays to her husband. By this time, Darwin was seen less as a dangerous revolutionary than as a grand old man of science, revered by the nation. His view of himself was much more modest and, even in old age, he went on working and learning. In the last year of his life, he taught himself how to prepare sections of roots and leaves for examination under a microscope.

But, among scientists, the climate of opinion was changing fast, in support of Darwinism. The idea of evolution – applying to all living things – had become easier and easier to accept. Huxley himself, in 1863, had published a book called *Evidence of Man's Place in Nature.* In many ways, the battle over humanity's origins had been fought and won before Darwin started to write his own *Descent.*

Serenely, he went straight on to his next big work, on the ways humans and animals express emotion. Here, too, Darwin found several expressions and gestures that they had in common.

The final years

Darwin spent the last ten years of his life much as he'd spent all the thirty years before: mainly at Down House, working, and enjoying the company of his family and much-loved pets. Strangely, his troubled health began to improve. He did not seem to be ill any more – just tired. His life's work was completed. The subject that had haunted him for so long had, at last, been defined, put into words, launched upon the world. It could go its own way now. And he would go his: studying the movement of earthworms, and writing his autobiography.

At the end of 1881, he had a heart attack. He recovered, but the following spring, when he was seventy-three years old, he had another – and then a third. In the afternoon of April 19, 1882, Charles Darwin died.

At first, Emma and his children wanted him to be buried in the little village church close by. But the public – Parliament, scientists, press – thought otherwise, and the family gave way. On April 26, 1882, as a mark of the deepest national respect, the reluctant enemy of the Church was buried in Westminster Abbey in London.

Darwinism evolves

In 1904, less than quarter of a century after Darwin died, a German writer named Dennert published his own views on evolution. The title he gave them was *At the Deathbed of Darwinism.*

The deathbed? Did Darwin's views only outlive their great creator by twenty-two years? What, after the success of the 1870s, had happened?

In fact, one part of Darwin's theory – the idea that species changed and evolved – was in perfect health. Few now disagreed with it. But many, like Dennert, still disagreed with the idea of natural selection, and hoped they could argue it out of existence.

For a while, it looked as if they might succeed. But then, thanks to work done by other scientists, the arguments of the anti-Darwinists began to be discredited. And, by the 1940s, Darwin's theory had taken a new, reshaped place in the explanation of how life works. Darwinism, far from being dead, was itself evolving: taking on new forms.

Bringing findings together

Scientists call this new explanation the "evolutionary synthesis". The name was made famous in a book by Sir Julian Huxley, the grandson of

"No fact in the long history of the world is so startling as the wide and repeated exterminations of its inhabitants."

Charles Darwin.

The workings of heredity, as observed by the monk Gregor Mendel. By crossing strains of garden pea, Mendel studied how traits were handed on from one generation of living things to the next. Special traits that he studied included the tallness of the pea plants, the smoothness of the peas' skin, and – as shown here – their shade. Each pea in the diagram is shown with a pair of traits: one inherited from each of its parents.

Parents   1st Generation   2nd Generation

Mendel found that, if he crossed a yellow pea with a green pea, all the offspring had yellow peas. But, if two of these plants were interbred, a quarter of their seedlings would have green peas. Findings like these showed two things. The first was that the traits of parents combined in their offspring. However, they did not blend; a yellow/green pea cross did not come out as a greenish-yellow! The second was that some characteristics – like tallness, or the shade yellow – were "dominant". Peas with the yellow factor in their genetic make-up were always yellow, even if the green factor was also present.

Darwin's old friend. But "synthesis" means "bringing together", and the evolutionary synthesis is based on the findings of many scientists, working in many different fields.

The first of them all was the monk Gregor Mendel, who had read Darwin. His discoveries in genetics were ignored for many years, then rediscovered in 1900. Mendel discovered the patterns by which living creatures hand on their features from one generation to the next. If, for instance, tall peas were crossed with dwarf ones, all the hybrids were tall. But, if two of these tall hybrids were then crossed, a quarter of their offspring would be dwarf. Mendel worked out why this happened. But he couldn't work out *what* the plants were handing on to each other: what shape that "factor" for tallness or dwarfness took.

The white-eyed flies

The scientists who studied his work included an American zoologist, Thomas Hunt Morgan. Working with fast-breeding fruit flies, he began to study mutations: suddenly-occurring differences in individual members of a species. In 1910, he found he could breed a new strain of flies with white eyes.

He also found that all the white-eyed flies were male; the "white-eye factor" was linked to its owner's sex.

From here, Morgan was able to identify the "factor" itself, now called a gene. At least, he could say where in the flies' bodies it was: he could show that these basic building blocks of heredity lay on the thread-like chromosomes present in the flies' body cells. It was a big step forward – but, in many other ways, genes still remained a mystery.

Genes and DNA

Chromosomes, genes, the mathematics of natural selection: it was all beginning to add up. As more and more details emerged of how life functioned, people realized that Darwin's findings and Mendel's fitted together.

Julian Huxley's book appeared in 1942. It was soon followed by further key developments. Scientists studying DNA, a chemical found in chromosomes, discovered that this was the "messenger" they were looking for. It was the substance that, transmitted from one generation to the next, handed on the instructions of heredity. DNA, in fact, was made of genes.

With the 1960s, the genetic code – the chemical code in which heredity's instructions were expressed – began to be cracked. And it was discovered that this code was the same for all living creatures.

Darwin's tentative conclusion that all organisms were "descended from some one prototype" had received the most unexpected backing.

The ideas live on

Every step in the discovery of how life works throws new light on the theory of evolution. But, even today, scientists insist that it *remains* a theory: usually the time-scales involved are too big to allow us to produce final, total proof.

For this reason, controversy over Darwinism continues. In the scientific world, new ideas about evolution are put forward all the time. Meanwhile, some people still oppose evolution on religious

"Charles Darwin is the father of modern biology. His ideas remain at the heart of it."
Colin Tudge, speaking on BBC Radio, July 30, 1989.

"Some check is constantly preventing the too-rapid increase of every organised being left in a state of nature. The supply of food, on average, remains constant; yet the tendency in every animal to increase by propagation is geometrical.... In a species long established, any great increase in numbers is obviously impossible, and must be checked by some means."
Charles Darwin.

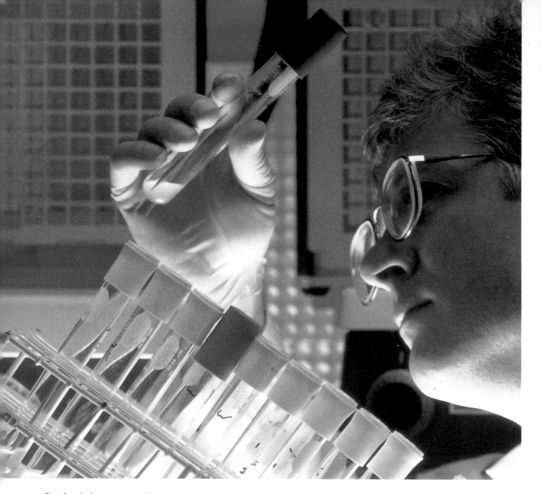

In the laboratory, the story continues. According to some of the latest thinking on evolution, highly intelligent beings – like humans – can bypass the "survival of the fittest" law. Their brains allow them to adapt to any circumstances that come along. Genetic evolution is replaced by cultural evolution, or learning, which works much faster. Mammals have already evolved faster than fishes and reptiles; who knows what the future will bring?

grounds. Between the wars, for instance, teachers in the state of Tennessee in the U.S.A. were banned from teaching that humans were not made in the image of God, but descended from lower forms of life. This so-called "Monkey Law" was only repealed in 1967. And, in the 1970s, some school-children in the United States were still using biology textbooks that did not mention the word "evolution".

But, as Darwin himself realized 150 years ago, controversy and his theory are tightly bound together. The fact that people are still arguing over it is proof of its importance. Darwin's legacy to us has changed over the years, but the ideas he worked out so painfully still resound in our lives and the way we think.

Important Dates

1809   February 12: Charles Robert Darwin is born in Shrewsbury, England.

1818   Darwin goes to Shrewsbury School as a boarder.

1825   Darwin goes to Edinburgh University to study medicine.

1826   Darwin reads his first scientific paper to the university natural history society.

1828   Charles Darwin goes to Cambridge University and graduates in 1831.

1831   August 29: Darwin, aged twenty-two, receives the invitation to join *HMS Beagle* as unpaid naturalist. Early in September, Darwin meets Captain FitzRoy and is accepted for the post.
December 27: The *Beagle* sets sail for South America.

1832-   The *Beagle* sails up and down the eastern coast of South America. The main
1834   ports of call include Salvador, Rio de Janeiro, Montevideo, and the Tierra del Fuego region. Darwin discovers his fossilized giants at Punta Alta, Argentina, in 1833.

1834   The *Beagle* enters the Pacific.

1835   September 15: After voyaging up the west coast of South America, the *Beagle* reaches the Galapagos Archipelago, and remains there until October 20.

1835-   The *Beagle* makes her homeward voyage, via New Zealand, Australia, the
1836   Indian Ocean, and the Cape of Good Hope. She arrives in England on October 2, 1836.

1837   Darwin takes lodgings in London. Inspired by his observations at Punta Alta and in the Galapagos, he starts studying the evolution of species. He begins to have health difficulties at the age of twenty-eight

1838   Darwin reads Malthus's *Population,* and sees the connection between evolution and the struggle of all species for survival.

1839   Charles Darwin marries his cousin, Emma Wedgwood. His health gets much worse. His *Journal* of the voyage is published.

1842   May: Darwin starts writing a pencil sketch of his species theory.
September: The Darwins move to Down House, Kent.

1844   Darwin writes a longer version of his species theory.

1846   Darwin starts his eight-year study of barnacles.

1856   Darwin begins to write his "big book", outlining his theory of evolution by natural selection.

1858   Darwin receives Wallace's letter. Both his early sketch of his theory and Wallace's paper are read to the Linnean Society. Darwin starts work on *The Origin of Species.*

1859   November 24: *The Origin of Species* is published in London.

1860   Professor T.H. Huxley, "Darwin's bulldog", vanquishes Bishop Wilberforce in a debate at Oxford, at the annual meeting of the British Association for the Advancement of Science.

1862 Darwin publishes his book on orchid pollination.

1864 The Copley Medal of the Royal Society is awarded to Darwin for his work on geology, zoology and botany.

1868 Darwin publishes his *Variation of Animals and Plants under Domestication*.

1871 *The Descent of Man* is published.

1872 Darwin publishes his *Expression of the Emotions in Man and Animals*.

1881 Darwin, aged seventy-two, publishes his last book, *The Formation of Vegetable Mould, Through the Action of Worms*.
December: While visiting a friend in London, he has a heart attack.

1882 April 19: Charles Darwin dies at Down, aged seventy-three.
April 26: As a mark of national respect, Charles Darwin is buried at Westminster Abbey in London.

Further reading

Attenborough, David: *Life on Earth,* Collins/British Broadcasting Corporation, London, 1979.

Burton, Robert & Maurice: *Beginnings of Life,* Orbis, 1986.

Clark, Ronald W.: *The Survival of Charles Darwin – a Biography of a Man and an Idea,* Weidenfeld and Nicolson, London, 1985. [Massive, but extremely readable.]

Fletcher, F.D.: *Darwin,* Shire Publications, London, 1975.

Marshall Cavendish Learning System: Man and Medicine *Heredity, Family and Society,* Marshall Cavendish, London, 1968.

Moorehead, Alan: *Darwin and the Beagle,* Hamish Hamilton, London, 1969. [Excellent account of the *Beagle* voyage, and its aftermath.]

Raverat, Gwen: *Period Piece: a Cambridge Childhood,* Faber, London, 1952. [Gwen Raverat was one of Darwin's grandchildren. It contains a brilliant (and very funny) description of Darwin family life.]

Skelton, Renee: *Charles Darwin,* Barron's Educational, USA, 1987.

Sully, Nina: *Looking at Genetics,* Batsford, 1985.

Taylor, Ron: *Evolution,* Macdonald Educational, London, 1978.

Scientific Terms

Archaeopteryx: The earliest form of bird yet discovered, combining features of both birds and reptiles. *Fossil* specimens date from over a hundred million years ago.

Archipelago: The technical name for a group of islands.

Biology: The study of living things.

Botany: The scientific study of plant life.

Capybara: The world's largest living rodent. Capybaras grow to about four feet long. They live on the banks of lakes and rivers in South America, and have partly webbed feet.

Cell: A minute block of jelly-like substance, enclosed in a membrane. It is the basic unit out of which all living organisms are made.

Chromosomes: The thread-like structures found within the nucleus of a cell. Each species has its own chromosome count. In humans it is forty-six; in the flies Thomas Hunt Morgan studied, it is four. As an organism grows, and its cells increase by dividing themselves into two, the chromosomes divide as well. Because of this, the new cells have exactly the same number of chromosomes as the "parent" ones.

Creationism: The belief that all the world's species were made by God during the six-day period of Creation described in the Christian Bible, and that the forms they were made in have not changed since.

Darwinism: The theory that new species evolve through natural selection. Often used just to mean "evolutionism".

DNA: The abbreviation for deoxyribonucleic acid, the chemical found inside chromosomes that carries the genetic instructions for the way cells should develop.

Evolution: The process by which something gradually develops into something different and new; can be used of ideas and relationships, as well as of living things. According to the theory of evolution, the world's species have developed from species that existed earlier. This idea was in direct contradiction to the views of the *creationists.* "Evolutionists" were scientists who rejected the *creationist* view and believed that evolution did take place.

"Factor" (of heredity): The earlier name for *gene.*

Fossil: The buried remains of once-living creatures preserved in some form by the action of the earth. Many fossils, like skeletons and tree-stumps, have been preserved by being turned into stone.

Genes: The chemical instructions, carried on the *DNA* in the *chromosomes,* by which parents pass on their characteristics to their young. These instructions are expressed in an intricate chemical code.

Geology: The study of earth formations.

Heredity: The handing on of characteristics from parents to offspring. Darwin used the word "inheritance" to mean the same thing. A feature that is handed on like this is called "hereditary".

Hybrid: The offspring produced by breeding different varieties of animals or plants.

Modify, modification: Words often used by Darwin to mean "evolve" and *evolution.* He used "transmutation" in the same way.

Molecule: A minute particle of matter, made up of two or more kinds of atoms.

Natural history: The name that, in Darwin's time, was given to the scientific study of plants and animals.

Natural selection: The process by which individual organisms that are specially well-equipped to exploit their surroundings hand on their special characteristics to increasing numbers of descendants, finally giving rise to a new species in which all members share the original special feature. This was the core of Darwin's thinking.

Ornithology: The scientific study of birds.

Species: A group of organisms that are alike, and that can produce offspring that are themselves capable of producing offspring. A "genus" consists of a group of similar species. The two iguana species that Darwin found in the Galapagos both belonged to the genus *Amblyrhynchus.*

Variety: A group of distinctive – and closely similar – organisms within a single species. A Siamese cat and a long-haired Persian are both varieties of the species *Felis catus.* Different species cannot interbreed and produce fertile young, but different varieties within the same species can.

Zoology: The scientific study of animal life.

Index